MW01033462

FROM THE WATER'S EDGE

A collection of poetry written while wandering

Shun P. Writes

From the Waters' Edge – A collection of poetry written while wandering Copyright © 2019 by Shun P. Writes. All Rights Reserved.

All rights reserved. No part of this book may be reproduced in any form or by any electronic or mechanical means including information storage and retrieval systems, without permission in writing from the author. The only exception is by a reviewer, who may quote short excerpts in a review.

Cover designed by Cover Designer

This book is a work of original poetry. Names, characters, places, and incidents either are products of the author's imagination or are used fictitiously. Any resemblance to actual persons, living or dead, events, or locales is entirely coincidental.

Shun P. Writes
Visit my website at www.shunpwrites.com

Printed in the United States of America

First Printing: July 2019
EditCat Consulting, Inc.

ISBN- 9781077506992

For my Father, Alexander Patterson Sr.

TABLE OF CONTENTS

PREFACE

Most of these poems were written as I walked the trails of forests and state parks of Maryland and stood on the shores of several inspirational bodies of water in the region... hence the name of this book. These poems touch on the issues of racism and injustice and run the gamut of emotions from melancholy and introspection to the realities of joy and pain.

The undercurrent that flows throughout each piece, however, is a theme of faith and redemption. But, in wandering these paths my dark spaces were illuminated, my purpose made clear, and I was able break free from my greatest enemy, myself.

That being said – I am honored that you have chosen to accompany me on this path.

TAKING THE MANTLE

I became my
Father
on what seems
like yesterday –

without his flaws
but
regurgitating
and
drowning in mine.

Adrift in bewilderment
musing silently
that
it
is
all
in my mind –
or perhaps
by design
this shell from
which I came.

But –

starkly, sharply, divergently
opposite –
but the same.

Time refines
bringing the legions –
compare and contrast
past, present, future.

Summarily
the echoes
of
acknowledgement
of
what is –
serving as
the suture
to join;
not to
duplicate.

Your failures
are
my successes
your shortcomings
my lessons
your steps
my protection.

Am I your
legacy?

Will you
marvel
or grimace
at what
you have wrought?

You taught me
that life's battles
are worth
the cost.

As I
become you.

A father
who
repeats –

the cycle
fueling the fire
to aspire higher
in adoration
at what
I have wrought.

* * *

PROVIDENCE SENT – FOR YOU MOMMA

Rendition of the
unconditional.
Unequivocally
essential.

Unlike the sun
that sets
in the west –

Providence beget
an implement
that was
love.

Unadulterated
tendered freely
encapsulated in
steely resolve
reminiscent
of
Gibraltar - never faltering.

Overdelivering -
is that which comprises
your structure
in abundance.

Adoration

of a selflessness
that was
evinced
ever since –
I was born.

You are that
contagious light
illuminating the
darkness as
I labor to be worthy.

No.
Me.
Without you.

Those torrential seas
made calm
by the manifestation of grace –
Momma.

* * *

I CAN'T BREATHE

Is feeling
powerless –
tantamount.

To silence –
irrelevance.
Death?

I can't breathe.

Is feeling.
As if my
countenance
is inconsequential?

I can't breathe.

Minimized
hypnotized –
by
the venom
of what is –
as it
metastasizes.

I can't breathe.

Raging

against the duality
that entertains and suffocates –
in short order.

I can't breathe.

Laughter masks the pain.
As I stand.
In stationary oscillation
weary and haggard
I fall –
Because.

I can't breathe.

* * *

WHO I IS?

___

Is who I is –
dismay you –
jade and
dissuade
making you feel
some type of way?

I could care less –
because I spit shit –

while my eloquence
is minimized
and humanity
subsequently euthanized.

You look in
my eyes
casually –

seeing
savagery
absconding
into the depths
of dismissiveness –

being better to
live there
versus
living in the periphery
of being equal –

playing victim
to the centrifugal force
of ignorance
that convinces the blind
that there
is no sequel.

Like the properties
of a quasar
or Black Hole
relegated to the edges

of our
understanding –
those galaxies
where
no light escapes
through the peephole –

you see me
as you are –
an unredemptive
lost soul in repose.

While the tacit realization
of what is –
makes
the blood run cold.

Lies become
truth
invective begetting a
false pride –
that leaves the legions
hypnotized
rancid and dead inside.

* * *

THE OTHERNESS

Multiple degrees
suits
mirror polished
shoes and boots –
seamless
coordination
assimilation
migration through
layers of
organizations and
business
administrations.

After all is said
and done –
it
matters
little to none.

Seldom cheered
partial
to being feared
like one
wielding a gun.

As the burdened
wrestle with the
profundity of hate.

* * *

THAT UNBENDING SKIN

It is like
an omnipresent effort –
being a pawn
in a game –
of humanity being
consistently
inconsistent.

That skin
that won't bend –
subjected to the duality
of avoiding
consecutive blows
targeted to concurrently impact
the body and soul.

If it makes you
uncomfortable
hearing about it –

imagine the cruel irony
of having to
go through it?

Live it.

Taste it.
Feel it.
Hear it.
Be seen.
Not heard.
Told.
To get over it.

Told.

That it is okay
while the acidity
of not having
to know –

ferments into the
pungent swill of ignorance
only to eat
away at the foundation.

Extrapolate that over
the course of a lifetime.
Those raging rapids
of otherness –
clashing against
colossus of invective
in waters that
won't be stilled.

* * *

IN IVORY TOWERS

Those who wield
darkened countenances
in ivory towers –

shower the gathered
with hollow platitudes
that euthanizes **humanity**
while **killing** the body.

In the effort to secure
the elusive prize –

that is **their**
absolution of the encumbrance
of guilt.

* * *

PARALLEL PLANES

The militancy of faith
goes unheralded –
when showers dampen resolve
and canyons fill
with the rapid waters
of the morose

who tender alms of
idolatry
to those
wielding power
in their domicile.

The indignity of
fools
drowning in tears
juxtaposed
with the blessed
who recline
on parallel planes
of grace –
where
dysfunction kneels
to
the ever present militance
of omnipotence.

* * *

THOSE MELANCHOLY MELODIES

When those
melodies are lost.

It seems as
if I cry

all the time –
as the rooms within
my heart are dark
missing it –

wrestling mightily
at night
waiting for sleep
that does not come –
as my sorrows
serve as a tomb.

The dead of silence
summarily interrupted –
by the unmelodious
tapping of tears
hitting the floor –
light creeping in
under the door
calling out –
as muffled shouts
leave no echo.

Pangs of loneliness
fueled by
notions of nothingness –
when karma calls
extracting the price
while I protest –
it isn't right.

Claiming victim

when truth revels
in the light –
with affliction
being the author
of the pain
which darkens
my visage –
driving me
down a long road
to a destination
of insanity –

torturous blows
to ego serve
as gravitational elements
of humility.

In that darkness –
lies the revelatory truths
denied to haughty eyes
that despised
the nectar oozing
from ethereal plains –
incalculable changes
rearrangement
containment
the fires of contradictions –
acquiesce to an extinction
earned as the fire
burns hotter –
begging me
to step through

in a rite of purification.

But –
as the echoes
of my muffled shouts
providentially echo back
to that light
under the door –
that illumination
was grace
compelling me
to the floor –
to get low
in acknowledgement
from whence it all flows.

Baptized by tears
laying claim
to greater destination
serving a God
mightier than
the facade of melancholy
tendering the
that prized possession
the offer –
of a faith
which harkens to
a sweeter melody.

* * *

THE UNCOMMON

Those
twisting paths of
allurement –
leading to
a beauty
that cannot
be entombed.

Enlisting disciples
on ethereal calls –
giving testament
to segues
pauses
indictments
realizations
of the uncommon.

Vibrations of the
unrequited
those owners
of
passions
that lie
prostrate
on a pyre

waiting to be
consumed
by their fire.

* * *

CAVALCADES OF RADIANCE

Empyreal notions
potions enchantments –
incantations providing fuel
for perspiration
heart palpitations
that which harkens –
bombardments into
cavalcades of radiance
and dalliances of thought
as the gathered clamour
desirous to be near –
to procure
the simple
yet untenable –
kiss.

* * *

FORSAKEN ADDICTION

A pull –
like the
Earth to the Moon.

The Moon to the tides –
a magnet to metal.

A visage which –
runs contrary to the laws of
physics –

psychic; supernatural; otherworldly.

But –
terrestrial in origin.

But when starved
of the embrace
that
affords
nourishment –
that
foraging
does
not
supply.

It leaves one
barren, hollowed and emaciated
inside.

Only to be discarded –
as a useless vessel.

* * *

COMMUNION OF FREQUENCIES

Frequencies that harken
onto dimensions unmentioned
a love unseen
but palatable –
hearts in communion
endeavoring in a sensation
the edification
of what is congealed
in the realm
of the real
the residency of passions –
sealed
entombed –
never to be consumed.

* * *

FALSE ALLEGIANCES

Those barren landscapes
laid waste -
inhabitants speaking in
hollow inflections.

Jilted egos orbiting -
a dead star.

Going through the motions
fortified by the potion -
a notion of self-worth.

Pushing back against
those vicious lies -
casting aside
misplaced allegiances -
to take on
mandates that
make the Earth shake.
Clouds on horizon
give testament -
cowardice in flight
of the chosen
turning tail to
run like Jonah.

Hiding from
the omnipotence of purpose -

guilty of placing
faith
in the wrong places.

Swallowed whole –
fermenting in the
belly of that
which they could not
elude.

Penance in the void
redemption gifted
priorities shifted
knees on ground
beholding the power
of the weight
lifted.

* * *

THE REVELATION

Sanctimonious exhortations.
echo loudly.
Saying nothing.

Outside, looking in.
Far too weary.
To pretend

or deny –
the power
manifested
when the hour of
cognizance calls.

Leaving in its wake
boundaries and foundations
consummated and lusting
for truth
versus
fictitious ramblings.

While keeping company
in concert
with contradictions –
dalliances of morality
preening, strutting
admirably resolute
and blissfully ignorant.

While –
denying
the finality of defeat.
As lies –
Illusion
perusal.

Laid bare to
revelation of the fact...

The charlatan.

Revealed
rendered and made plain
its countenance.

Never to be taken back.

Curtain raised –
exit.
Stage left.
Silence –
no pause for applause.

* * *

WHEN TEARS HIT GROUND

That tome
of sorrow
as tears
hit ground
shaking the foundations
of the soul
like a baritone –
time rendered
not a gift –
but as a loan
that reminder given
when the Almighty

calls his children home –
the love of those
who knew you –
serving as
segues to
heaven –
positioned
in the spaces
of grace –
leaving the willing
in the wake
that is the search
for God's face.

THE FALLEN

Walls closing in
push back.

Stumble.

Once, twice, thrice
sprawling onto
Gaia.
Terra.

Laying prostrate
implored

galvanized
and
divorced
from the hoarseness of defeat.

Standing up –
stronger backs,
not lighter burdens
emboldened
to pull the curtains back.

For
empowerment –
not weakness
that leaves
one in pieces
the tell-tale signs

creases of stress
tells best
but
blesses better
giving way to peace of mind
in time.

* * *

THOSE UNWORTHY HANDS

Radiance
which illuminates
the vacuous ruins
of that
which once stood
tall.

There stands
the illusion of wreckage.
That light flowing
through the cracks –

barren caverns where
hope once flowed
to a segue
of purpose.

Restorative notions
running contrary
to stagnation –
stumbling down an
embankment
of haunting indignity
so close –
yet so far
while tortuously informed
of
not being able

to touch it –
that oasis of
beauty that
fortifies the confines.
While the unworthy
stand with
their
hands outstretched.

* * *

TAKEN AWAY

Pain and emptiness
tear stained trails
aching hearts–
echoes that don't answer.
A pain that portends
can't be ignored
when subservient to
those pangs
of that which
is taken away –
on knees that
only bend
in deference
to the contours of faith.

AS THE WEARY SEARCH

Dutifully searching
for the amorous inclinations
of what is.
Not knowing
what, will, would, could, should
be procured.

As muffled cries
echo back unanswered
radiating
a fictitious confidence
of futility.

Walking in concert with
hesitancy
as companion.

Uneven steps
languishing at the precipice
of battle –

no Excalibur
forged in the
resplendent grace
of the most High.

My conferences
with the Lord.
He, she, divine presence.

Heaven sent, beneficent
no shouts, but whispers
stories told.

Burdens dropped
inspirations lifted –
solace gifted
to me.

The wretched.
Blatantly unworthy –
but protected.

* * *

THOSE RISING TIDES

Hypocrisy hides
under a cover
of haughtiness –
killing slowly.

Cutting against
the grain

notwithstanding
naivete.

To pain
disguised as
majestic airs –

while reality
leaves a trail
of desolation
in its wake.

Weathering
torrential storms
of
teary eyes
and thunderous moans.

But.

Electing
to stand taut
against the onslaught.

Not knowing when
but –
knowing how.

Rising celestially
like the sun
in East.

Defeat stands
emboldened
certain
of its undertaking
postulating victory –

neglecting the
rising tides of grace.

As necks crane
ears discern
eyes strain –
to acquiescence
on bended knee.

Hypocrisy flees –
knowing it was
the Almighty
enveloping me.

* * *

UNCONSECRATED SPACES

Dark places
spaces
consumed by weights
unconsecrated –

while
no protection
is proffered
from those spirits -
disaffection and defeat.

Wanderers in the fields
where notions of
value are derelict -
non-existent and hollow.

Wistful
entreaties
are met with
volleys -
those closed fists
of rejection
unable to surmise –

hypnotized by muffled cries
only to be euthanized –

bleeding out
from within -
those fractured
shards of self
submerged beneath
the watery depths -
those oceans of
their salty tears.

* * *

COWARDICE OF IGNORANCE

Behind the veil
lurks
a masquerading eloquence
of faux bravery
its ugliness
revealed.

Cowardice of ignorance
rigidity of thought
paucity of empathy.

The partitioning of the same
by the same –
a prerequisite to –
a crying shame.

THE CONTAGION

Contagiously so
complacency is.

Serving as the foil

for
the endemic nature
of
"just enough to get by".
Getting high
off of that
which
masquerades
as steps forward.

Obliviously –
deaf to the call
of resolve
as the siren song of
is more than enough
to leave the
feebleminded stranded
on the shores.

* * *

THE LONGING

The pestilence
of
ignorance
and
the
propensity

of
its
preference
running counter
to
deference
and
the
esteem
harboured by
worshipful
inclinations.

The yearning for a sensation
induced by those
who aspire for
the proverbial fire –
of something greater.

* * *

SUPPOSITION OF THE BROKEN

Those paths that wind
as the willing search
for the divine –
pushing back against
the supposition
that the broken
cannot be refined.

* * *

ON THE RAILS

Life encased
in recollections
those sections
predilections
of what was.

Those rails
encompassing
tales –
days past
rash decisions
elemental forces
procuring divorces
against competing realities.

Skylines of youth
juxtaposed against
jaded notions
of our present –
our presence
reeking
of a truth
dispersed
running
counter to

a worth embedded
along the
path of myopic
entanglements.

Past is future
future is past
sutures in time
lending to
foundational components
of design
which is
refinement –

segues
of
resignation
to a destination
where frustrations
don't vacation –
wisdom upends
as the Almighty
compels knees
to bend.

Our fares tendered
for the admission
onto a train
of divine intervention.

* * *

CRIES OF THE FAITHFUL

Why is it that
you have taken
so long to use me?
Is it because
I have
abused
misconstrued
extrapolated
and deviated
from the covenants
of grace?

Wondering if
there is a trace of providence
left that burns within?

To extinguish my sins
on knees that bend
as my convictions
cry out
with a diction
born of humility
forged in
the futility
of my failures
while
those

consequences
of recalcitrance
left me for dead.

But –
instead of
decomposition –
the unworthy
was
repositioned
on the winding paths
of a salvation
sought
by the
forsaken
now
rewarded for their
inclinations
of keeping pace
with grace.

* * *

DEAF WITH APPRECIATION

The world deafens me
with its static.
While...
The solace of silence

awakens
that which was dormant.

Looking up
to the sky
thirsting for intervention
but
rewarded with dissension.
Insanity thrives
tears dry
moans muffled
and I'm inclined
repressing, compressing
otherwise keeping
it inside.
But...
Earnestly searching
for the elusive
to be
reprieved, pardoned
longing for the
ecstasy of a burden
lifted from weary limbs.
Only to discover
that appreciation
will soon
eclipse the struggle.

* * *

ON THE CUSP

Notions of worth
truncated and scattered –
victims of the wind.

As the unworthy wander
on the winding
trails of disaffection
desirous to hold
or be held –

reaching out
on a cusp of a touch
not be had –

spurned and relegated
convicted and sentenced
to die of a thirst –

that will not
be quenched.

* * *

PRESCRIPTION OF THE LONELY

Absence of touch
a prescription of indifference
as the lonely languish
on the shores –

as their mournful wails
are drowned out –

by the
rivers replenished with
the torrential storms of
tears that won't dry.

* * *

THE ART OF BEING STILL

Minimizing our humanity
that cacophony of contradictions
in conflict with
reflections that vibrate –
subjecting me to their
protection.
Allowing me
to thrive and not thrash

45

purge not submerge -
not perfection but humility
evolution not pollution
of the spirit.
Being still
so that I can hear it.

* * *

NOTE TO SOUL

We place our
souls in repose
when we pursue goals
that will never
leave us whole.

* * *

To be continued in:

Allusions to Life: Reflections of an Ancestor Whisperer

Made in the USA
Lexington, KY
22 November 2019

57447034R00034